the extreme sports collection

Wakeboarding!
throw a tantrum

Chris Hayhurst

rosen publishing group's

rosen central

new york

Wakeboarding! : throw a tantrum

T 29004

Published in 2000 by The Rosen Publishing Group, Inc.
29 East 21st Street, New York, NY 10010

First Edition

Library of Congress Cataloging-in-Publication Data

Hayhurst, Chris.
    Wakeboarding! throw a tantrum / by Chris Hayhurst. — 1st ed.
        p.   cm. — (The extreme sports collection)
    Includes bibliographical references (p. 60) and index.
    Summary: Describes the history, equipment, techniques, and safety measures of wakeboarding, which is a combination of waterskiing and snowboarding.
    ISBN 0-8239-3008-4
    1. Wakeboarding Juvenile literature.   [1. Wakeboarding.] I. Title.   II. Series.
GV840.W34H39   2000
797.3'2—dc21   99-16256
                                                                        CIP
                                                                        AP

Manufactured in the United States of America

contents

1 What's Extreme?
4

2 From Skurfers to Wakeboards
9

3 Where Do I Start?
16

4 Safe Boarding
20

5 Extreme Gear
25

6 Tips and Tricks
32

7 Competition
47

52 X-Planations   60 Extreme Reading
54 Extreme Info   62 Index
57 Where to Play   64 Credits

What's Extreme?

Let's get something straight: What's extreme to you might not be extreme to the next person. And what's extreme to that person might be tame to you. You see, the idea of "extreme" is relative. It means something different for everybody.

One thing everyone can agree on, however, is that when it comes to extreme sports, wakeboarding—a sort of combination of waterskiing and snowboarding—definitely qualifies. As wakeboarders are towed behind motorboats at speeds of twenty miles per hour or more, they can test their athletic limits with long, hard cuts across the

Leslie Kent does a backside roll.

water, nifty spins, big jumps, air rolls, tantrums, and other tricks. Whatever a wakeboarder tries is limited only by his or her imagination.

Wakeboarding is a fairly new sport. Just a few years ago, if you wakeboarded at all, you were extreme. If you mentioned the sport, it was likely that no one would know what you were talking about. You were living on the edge. You were extreme just because you were different.

Today it's not that simple. Wakeboarding is the fastest growing water sport in America. To be an extreme wakeboarder nowadays, you not only have to have a wakeboard, but you also have to know how to use it to do wild tricks. You have to know not only how to ride but how to do 360-degree spins, flips, and rolls.

Brannan Johnson competes at the 1998 Extreme Games in Sydney, Australia.

You have to launch yourself—and your board—over the waves and into the air. Then you have to land. And you have to do it in style. That's extreme.

Today there are the X Games, a sort of miniature Olympics for extreme sports. Athletes from around the world gather for this event to show just how extreme they can be. They climb ice walls; race down slippery, snow-covered ski slopes on mountain bikes; and jump out of airplanes with skateboards strapped to their feet. They compete to see who can grab the biggest air, who can hit the highest speeds, and who can perform the most difficult stunts. The winners are given gold medals and the title of "Most Extreme Athlete on the Planet." Most extreme, that is, until the next X Games, when new athletes will redefine what it means to be extreme.

Extreme Beginnings

The first Extreme Games, later known as the X Games, were held in 1995 in Rhode Island and attracted more than 350 world-class athletes. That year the events included bungee jumping, barefoot water-ski jumping, kite skiing, windsurfing, skysurfing, bicycle stunt riding, street luge, skateboarding, the Eco Challenge, and mountain biking. Wakeboarding was barely recognized as a sport at that point, and wasn't included. The next year, however, at the 1996 Summer X Games, wakeboarding was featured. And as anyone who witnessed the competition will tell you, the sport made a major splash!

Another version of extreme sports takes place behind-the-scenes, away from the glory that comes with television coverage and cheering crowds. These athletes prefer to play in the woods or on a quiet lake, alone with nature and the elements. They're the mountain climbers, the explorers, the recreational wakeboarders. They'll never get a gold medal for what they do, and they probably wouldn't want one anyway. They're doing what they do because they love it, not because it attracts a crowd.

Most people agree that for a sport to be extreme, it has to be difficult—at least for the

This could be you!

7

beginner. It must involve specialized skills and techniques. It also requires an adventurous attitude—the kind of attitude that says there are no limits. Whether this means carving high-speed turns on a smooth-as-glass lake, catching major air off a skyscraper-sized wake, or just getting into the water for the first time, it all depends on who you are and what you're willing, or not willing, to try.

Extreme sports can be dangerous, but being extreme doesn't mean being foolish or taking unnecessary risks. No wakeboarder wants to risk an injury that might mean never boarding again. You can be extreme and still follow safety rules.

If you think that you want to be extreme but you're not sure where to start, try wakeboarding. You'll find an adventure with every run. In wake-boarding, you can be as extreme as you want to be.

Opposite: Ryan Siebring carves a beautiful wakeboard turn, throwing a spray of water from the Wailua River, Hawaii.

Wake What?

The wakeboard looks a lot like a snowboard—it even has bindings on it to hold the rider's feet in place, just as a snowboard does. The major difference between a wakeboard and a snowboard is that the wakeboard is buoyant; it floats. The rider stands on the wakeboard and carves turns across the water. He or she does this while holding on to a rope that is attached to a moving boat. The wake—a long, wavy trail that the boat creates behind itself as it speeds through the water— provides a perfect ramp on which the rider can perform tricks. In expert competitions, boarders sometimes fly more than twenty feet into the air when they use the wake as a jump while airborne, they do somersaults, spins, and twists before landing back on the water. Now that's extreme!

The history of the sport of wakeboarding is a brief one. In fact, this sport has been around for only about fifteen years. In that short period of time, however, it has come a very long way. Today wakeboarding is the fastest growing water sport in America.

Wakeboarding would never have been invented if it weren't for the surfboard. In 1985 a California surfer named Tony Finn invented what he called a Skurfer. The Skurfer looked like a miniature

Brannan Johnson competes at the 1999 Wakeboard World Cup in Orlando, Florida.

surfboard but was used in a very different way: The surfboard was made to ride ocean waves, but the Skurfer was designed to move on flat water with the aid of a boat. On a lake, the wake takes the place of waves on the ocean.

The first Skurfers didn't have straps or any other way to attach the rider's feet to the board, so riders stood on it wherever they liked as a boat towed them across the water. It was very similar to surfing. That might sound like fun, but there were major problems with the setup. Without having their feet secured on the board, it was difficult for riders to keep from falling off. Even the seemingly simple act of making a turn across the wake involved an incredible amount of skill.Without straps, or bindings, to lock the feet down, the Skurfer was very hard to control.

Fortunately, Finn was friends with two windsurfers named Mike and Mark Pascoe. The Pascoes offered him the foot straps from their wind-surfing boards. Finn took the straps and figured out a way to attach them to his Skurfer. Because of that simple addition, the sport was changed forever.

With feet firmly anchored to the board, a rider could safely launch into the air by jumping the wake. Maneuvering on the water and in the air was a breeze. Riders could use their legs more efficiently to "edge" the sides of the board into the water, thereby causing it to turn. Mostly because of its similarity to waterskiing and snowboarding, this sport soon became known as skiboarding.

But skiboarding, like skurfing, continued to have its problems. The technology wasn't perfect, and the boards were still tough to ride. For one thing, they were usually very narrow, which made it hard to keep balanced. Also, the boards were too buoyant—they tended to float so well that simply getting started in the water was tremendously difficult.

A man named Herb O'Brien found a solution to these design problems. In 1989 O'Brien, who owned a water ski company, teamed up with some of the best surfboard builders in Hawaii to create a new board called the Hyperlite. The Hyperlite was less buoyant than earlier boards, so riders could hold it just beneath the surface as they started to move. That made it much

early board

twin-tip

easier to stand up once the ride began. The Hyperlite was also lightweight, and it had a high-tech bottom that allowed it to skim easily over the water. Most people agree that the Hyperlite was the first modern-day wakeboard.

Soon after the invention of the Hyperlite, other water ski companies began to produce similar boards. Over the years, the technology improved even further, and the sport grew in popularity. Before long, anybody with a boat and a big enough body of water could wakeboard.

By 1992 the sport had become so popular that the World Wakeboard Association (WWA), which was founded in 1989, began organizing professional wakeboarding events. The WWA is the worldwide governing body of the sport of wakeboarding. It has developed a standard set of rules for wakeboarding competitions.

Wakeboarding gained its fame in the world of extreme sports when it was included in the X Games in 1996. The competition was such a hit that it's been a part of every X Games since. In 1998 the Wakeboard World Cup had its first season. This international series of events for professionals

Boarder Bio

Parks Bonifay
Birthday: September 30, 1981
Hometown: Lake Alfred, Florida

Parks Bonifay has been one of the top wakeboarders in the world practically since his first competition. In 1996, he was named "Wakeboarder of the Year" by *Wake Boarding* magazine. That's not surprising, since he dominated the X Games and was the Pro Wakeboard Tour World Champion that year. Recently, Parks has had competition for the top ranking from his younger brother, Shane.

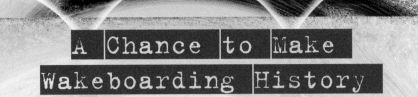

A Chance to Make Wakeboarding History

The 2004 Olympics, to be held in Athens, Greece, are just a few short years away. Although wakeboarding is not yet on the list of competitions to be staged that year, there's a good chance that wakeboarding will be included in the Games as part of the new Olympic waterskiing event. If that happens, you can bet that the top wakeboarders from around the world will go for Olympic gold. If wakeboarding is included, millions of people around the world will see the high-flying, gravity-defying, water-thrashing maneuvers that make the sport so extreme. You can be sure that nobody will be disappointed.

includes the top competitions—and competitors—in the world. The world champions of wakeboarding are crowned in the final event of the World Cup season. Many WWA events, including the Pro Wakeboard Tour, are now televised on ESPN and ESPN2 throughout the summer months, which helps the sport reach even more fans.

As wakeboarding enters the new millennium, everyone agrees: The sport is hot. In fact, it has become so popular that there's a good chance that it will be included in the 2004 Olympics in Athens, Greece. With both professional and amateur competitions on the rise, and more and more people discovering why the sport is so appealing, wakeboarding has become one of the athletic world's most extreme thrills.

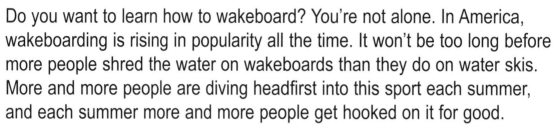

3

Where Do I Start?

Do you want to learn how to wakeboard? You're not alone. In America, wakeboarding is rising in popularity all the time. It won't be too long before more people shred the water on wakeboards than they do on water skis. More and more people are diving headfirst into this sport each summer, and each summer more and more people get hooked on it for good.

Getting started in wakeboarding isn't quite as easy as learning some other sports. One reason is that you can't wakeboard unless you have a big body of water. A good-sized lake will do. So will the ocean or a wide river. Second, motorboats must be allowed on that body of water, and they must

Extreme Fact
Nearly 1.5 million people participate in wakeboarding throughout the world, and more people try the sport every year.

be permitted to tow water-skiers. If the law allows water-skiers, chances are it will allow wakeboarders too. The last major obstacle to getting started in this sport is the fact that you need a boat. Boats are expensive—they can cost as much as or more than cars. They also need gas and someone to drive them.

Wakeboarding Paradise

Ask anybody in the world of wakeboarding where the best places are to ride, and you'll probably hear two names: California and Florida. Why those particular states? The water, of course! Both states are home to sunny weather, hundreds of miles of shoreline, and lots of warm water. But that doesn't mean you have to pack your bags just yet. You can wakeboard just about anywhere there's an open body of water. Almost any body of water will do, as long as it's large enough and deep enough to allow motorboats and there's plenty of room for you to make your turns. Lakes, rivers, the ocean—they're all fair game.

So there you are. Get yourself water and a boat, and keep the law on your side, and you'll be wakeboarding in no time. Sound impossible? Don't worry; it's not that hard.

Water can be found just about anywhere. Even if you happen to live in the desert, there's a good chance that a large body of water is not too far away. And in most places, you'll find the law to be wakeboarder-friendly. As for the boat, if you don't have one and don't know how you'll ever get your hands on one, don't worry. You can always hitch a tow on someone else's boat. Also, organized wakeboarding tournaments provide boats for the competitors. Even first-timers can catch rides at amateur wakeboarding tournaments.

Once you've got the technical stuff lined up, all you need is a wakeboard with bindings, a towrope, and a life jacket. Oh, and don't forget your bathing suit!

Where do you begin? Start with your friends and neighbors. Do you know any wakeboarders? If not, do you know people who water-ski?

They should be able to point you in the right direction, and they can definitely help you learn how the world of wakeboarding works. If you live in a town where waterskiing is popular, you should have no trouble finding the right people to get you started.

If you don't know any wakeboarders or water-skiers, try the phone book. Call around to water sports businesses, boat dealerships, and sporting-goods stores in your region. The people that work at these stores will know if there are any wakeboarding clubs in the area. They can also help you find equipment and introduce you to people who can get you started.

If none of these ideas work, give the World Wakeboard Association or *Wake Boarding* magazine a call. Tell them that you want to learn how to wakeboard, and ask how you can get the ball rolling. They can send you information on fun wakeboarding tournaments and beginner camps in your area.

Be warned: After you've given wakeboarding a try, you'll probably decide that you're going to devote the rest of your life to the sport. It's that addictive. If this happens, it's time to figure out what equipment you want to buy. You may already have a good idea of what you like just from wakeboarding with your friends. See chapter five for some other ideas on how to pick out the best gear for you.

Once you have everything you need, you're ready to go. Just remember that learning how to ride can be a difficult process. It may take several tries simply to figure out how to stand on the board without falling, let alone how to carve turns across the wake. Like most other sports, wakeboarding requires patience and, above all, practice. Give it all you've got!

4

Safe Boarding

wipeout

Wakeboarding sure looks like fun, but what happens when you wipe out? Well, usually you lose your grip on the towrope handle, skim across the water, maybe do a splashy somersault or two, and then come to a gentle rest. You end up bobbing in the water with your board, waiting for the boat to turn around and pick you up for another ride.

Sometimes, however, things don't go so smoothly. You might catch an edge and smack headfirst into the wake.

That can be both painful and possibly harmful. Or you might try a trick in midair and end up landing hard on your back. There is always a risk of injury. The truth is, wakeboarding can be a dangerous sport. The key to staying safe is understanding how to minimize the risks.

The most important thing you can do to ensure your safety is to wear a U.S. Coast Guard–approved Type III personal floatation device (PFD), better known as a life jacket. Even if you're a great swimmer, you should always wear your life jacket. If you're ever knocked out—and you just might be

if you bang your head on your board as you're pulling an air Raley—this handy device may save your life. Most states require wakeboarders to wear an approved life jacket.

Before you strap yourself into your life preserver, you should make sure that you've got the other safety details down. Take a look at your towrope. Is it tattered? If so, it may be time to get a new one. If the line breaks while you're being towed, it could whip back and hit you in the face. Now that would hurt!

Next, double-check your bindings.

Are they too tight? They should be snug, but not so tight that your feet won't release in a major wipeout. If they're too tight, you could easily break an ankle.

Now you can put on your life preserver. You're almost ready to go.

Before you begin your first ride, stretch out. Swim around a little to loosen up your leg, arm, and back muscles. A pulled muscle could mean no wakeboarding for several weeks. What a bummer!

Now that you're limber and you're sure that all your gear is in good shape, it's time to ride.

There should be at least two people in the boat: the driver, who will be steering the boat and keeping an eye on the water ahead, and a "spotter," who will be watching you as you board. The spotter's job is to tell the driver if you crash and to relay your signals to the driver. Give your spotter the OK sign, and swoosh! You're on your way!

Whoa, hold on! Not so fast. Your board should have come with a warning label indicating the maximum recommended speed at which it should be ridden. Make sure that you and your driver have agreed ahead of time what the boat's top speed will be. When you're starting out in wakeboarding, the boat's top speed shouldn't be much over fifteen miles per hour.

Speaking of boat speed . . . who's driving that boat, anyway? Make sure that your driver knows what he or she is doing. Many states offer safety education courses for all types of recreational boaters; it might be a good idea for you and your driver to take one. Most states require a license to operate a motorboat, and some won't give a boating license to anyone under a certain age (usually fourteen). Be sure to know the boating laws in your state.

Once you're moving, you'll need to keep a keen eye out for obstacles in, on, and around the water. If you're sharing the water with other boats, wakeboarders, and water-skiers, you and your driver should always be on the lookout. It's pretty much a no-brainer that both the driver of the boat and the wakeboarder should keep an eye out for swimmers. You should also keep your eyes peeled for docks, bridges, and other structures as well as the shore, sandbars, and rocks. There's nothing worse than smashing into an obstacle as you're skimming across the water at twenty miles per hour. Many smaller lakes have "no wake" rules that forbid motorboats to get too close to the shoreline. You should know and follow the rules of any body of water you're riding on.

Last but not least, board within your own personal limits. Above all, use caution and common sense. Never push yourself beyond what you can handle, and you'll be sure to stay safe and injury-free. Now let 'er rip!

Sign Language

When you're in the water and the boat engine is on, it can be impossible for you, your spotter, and your driver to talk. Use these hand signals instead.

Thumb up: Speed up!
Thumb down: Slow down!
Outstretched palm: Stop!
OK sign: Go!

slow down!

5 Extreme Gear

bindings

Getting the Gear

The equipment list for the wakeboarder is fairly short. All you really need—besides a boat, of course—is a board, bindings for your feet, a towline with a handle, and a life preserver. You'll also need a well-made bathing suit that won't get torn to shreds if you skip across the water in a wipeout.

handle

You won't want to just go out and buy all brand-new equipment. Gear is expensive, and you shouldn't buy anything until you know exactly what works best for you. Go out on the water with your wakeboarder friends and borrow their gear for a day or two. If you don't know any wakeboarders, rent equipment from a water sports shop. Better yet, "demo" some gear. When you demo, you pay a small fee to try out different brands of equipment. Once you're done with the demo, you get a credit toward anything you decide to buy. Often, amateur wakeboarding tournaments offer participants demo equipment that they can try for free.

life jacket

When you're ready to buy, make sure that you go over your options. It's wise to shop around. Consider buying used equipment. Buying used gear may not sound cool now, but it makes sense. You'll save money that you can put toward new and better equipment once you have a good idea of what you like.

Floating the Boat

One of the most important pieces of wakeboarding equipment is unfortunately also very expensive. You can't wakeboard without a boat. And boats, in case you haven't noticed, aren't exactly cheap. You'll need a boat that can hit about twenty miles per hour with a rider in tow. An inflatable dinghy won't do. Neither will a sailboat. You've got to have something with a big engine.

If a new boat is out of your league, look for a used boat. If a used boat is still too expensive, ride with your friends, find a marina where you can rent boats by the hour, or use the boats provided at friendly amateur tournaments. You don't have to let the boat get in the way of your learning to wakeboard.

Board Basics

Once you've got the boat issue taken care of, it's time to look at boards. There are all kinds of different wakeboards to choose from. The best boards are made of lightweight aluminum and carbon graphite. Older and cheaper models are made of polyurethane foam. These boards will still let you shred across the water, but they're heavier and slower than high-tech boards.

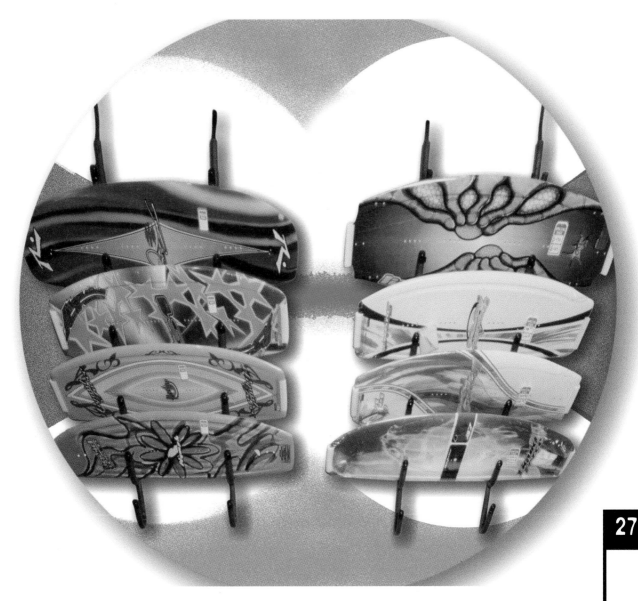

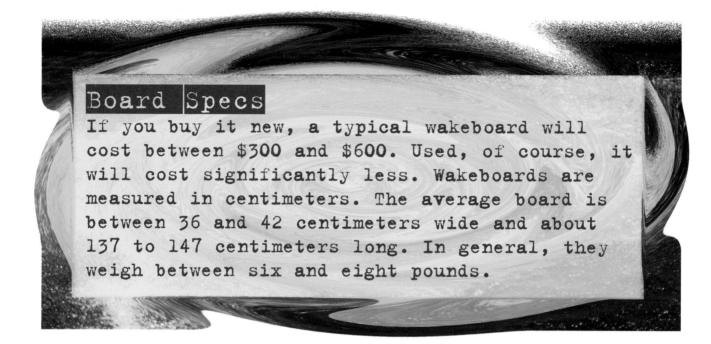

Board Specs

If you buy it new, a typical wakeboard will cost between $300 and $600. Used, of course, it will cost significantly less. Wakeboards are measured in centimeters. The average board is between 36 and 42 centimeters wide and about 137 to 147 centimeters long. In general, they weigh between six and eight pounds.

Most boards are just over four feet long and a little over one foot wide. The latest trend in wakeboards is the twin-tip design. Twin-tip boards are shaped the same in both the front and the back, with small fins on each end, allowing the rider to do tricks in either direction. This feature is useful if you like to ride "fakie," or backward.

There are a few things you should know when shopping for a board. The bigger and wider the board, the easier it is to ride. Big boards are more stable; you're less likely to fall off of one. However, because big boards are bulkier, they're not very good if you want to grab air or do technical maneuvers. For serious tricks, you need a smaller and thinner board. They're harder to control, but their light weight and low bulk allow for easy maneuverability.

Finally, check out the board's colors and graphics—you want to shred the wake in style.

Staying on Board

Unless you want to board as they did in the old days—and you probably don't—you'll need bindings to keep your feet in place. Bindings consist of two rubber booties attached to a piece of metal or plastic that is then fastened to the top of the wakeboard. The booties support your lower legs, ankles, and feet and allow you to lean and edge as you carve across the water. The bindings should be tight enough so that you won't come out of them when you do a trick, but loose enough to release your feet if you crash.

If your bindings are difficult to get your feet into, try this: Wet the bindings by soaking them briefly in the water, then put some dishwashing liquid or shampoo on them. Rub the soap into the bindings. Your feet should slide right in.

Make sure that the left and right bindings are equally tight. If they're not, you could find yourself with one foot stuck in a binding when you fall—and that can cause injuries.

These bindings are doing their job: keeping the wakeboarder on the board.

The Missing Link

The towrope is what links you and your board to the boat. This line is made of polyurethane and is forty-five to seventy feet long.

Wakeboarding ropes do not stretch easily, which gives the rider more control. A rope that stretches too much will spring back during tricks and throw the rider off balance. The towrope is fastened to the boat on one side and has a handle at the other end. The handle, which usually has a rubber grip, is what you hold on to as you ride. It is generally wider than standard water ski handles. Some riders wear special gloves for an even better grip.

You may see professional riders using braided wakeboarding ropes. These are not a necessity, but they do provide a better grip during tricks. They are also less likely to dig into your skin.

Other Gear and Gadgets

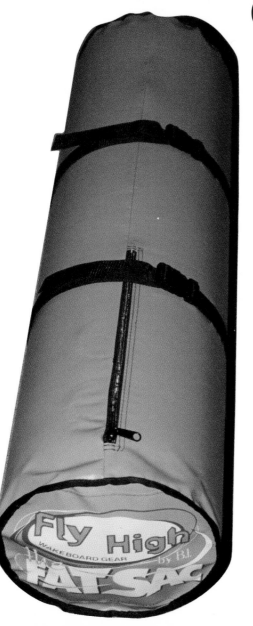

As you get better at wakeboarding, you'll probably want to buy more specialized equipment. A "fat sack," for instance, is an enormous bag filled with water that is dragged between the boarder and the boat. The bag weighs down the boat and creates a bigger wake—perfect for extreme tricks. An extended pylon is another piece of gear that many experienced wakeboarders use. This device holds the boat end of the towrope high over the boat so that when a rider gets big air off the wake, he or she can stay up longer. Finally, you may want to get a wet suit if you'll be riding in cold water. Even the best riders fall and get wet!

Boarder Bio

Shaun Murray
Born: April 28, 1976
Hometown: Orlando, Florida

When it comes to competition, Shaun Murray certainly knows how to win. Shaun has been one of the most consistent professional riders since he became the 1996 Pro Wakeboard Series Expression Session champ. Between that win and the 1999 season, he has taken top honors in many pro events, including the 1998 Wakeboard World Championships.

Wakeboarding is not an easy sport to learn. Sometimes it can be difficult just figuring out how to get up on the board and move across the water. If you know how to water-ski, you have got a head start on learning to wakeboard, but the two sports are not the same. Whether or not you can water-ski, though, once you pick up basic wakeboarding techniques, you'll probably find that the more difficult maneuvers—like how to catch big air off the wake—come fast. With some practice, you should soon have a handful of tricks that you can use anytime you go boarding.

Before you learn any tricks, you have to master the "easy" stuff—like how to get started when the boat begins to move. Getting started successfully takes a little practice.

Boarder Bio

Emily Copeland
Born: March 28, 1984
Hometown: Denver, Colorado

Emily is one of the hottest up-and-coming wakeboarders around. She's been competing for only a short time, but she has already been the Junior Women's National and World Champion on the Pro Wakeboard Tour.

goofy!

Are You Goofy or Regular?

If you ride with your right foot at the front of the board, you're a goofy-footer. If you ride left foot forward, you're a regular-footer. How do you know which way is best for you? Well, if you skateboard or snowboard, you already know; you should ride the same way when you wakeboard. If you've never ridden any kind of board before, try this trick: Stand up straight in the middle of a room and put your feet together. Have your best friend—someone you trust—push you from behind. The foot you put forward to stop yourself from falling should be your front foot on the wakeboard.

The first thing you need to do is get into the water with your board. As you float on the surface, put your feet into the booties. You might find it easier to put on your bindings while standing on a hard surface, such as the boat platform or the dock. In this case, get into the water carefully once your feet are in the bindings. Then float on your back with your knees bent. Keep the board between you and the boat. The board should face sideways, with

33

your toes pointed at the sky and the soles of your feet pointed right toward the back of the boat. Hold on to the towrope handle with both hands, keeping the rope draped over the middle of the board in a straight line toward the boat.

When you're ready to go, give the spotter the OK sign. Your driver will gun the engine, the boat will begin to move, and the rope will tighten. Relax your body, but hold on tight. And don't forget to keep your knees bent!

Before you know it, the boat will begin to pull your body up and out of the water. As you stand up, turn the board slowly so that it's pointed straight at the back of the boat. Away you go!

Tara Hamilton edging heelside.

Once you're moving, all you have to do is lean forward (toeside) or backward (heelside) to make the board turn. As you lean, keeping your weight on your toes or your heels, the board will go up onto one edge and begin to carve across the water. If you hold the turn long enough, you'll

eventually hit the
wake. Lift up your
feet as you hit the
wake, and you'll jump.
Hold on tight for big air!

A good trick for beginners to try is the
bunny hop. This jump doesn't require you to
use the wake, so it's easier for some novice
boarders to master. "Load" the rope by pulling on it to
create tension, and press your weight into the back of your
board at the same time. Then ease up on the rope. The release of tension combined with the downward pressure on the
board will give you a nice little hop. The techniques you learn in the
bunny hop will be helpful once you're ready to try some more advanced
jumps. Other beginner moves include crouching down and touching the
water, "surfing" the wake by turning up and down on it, and turning the
board ninety degrees on the water's surface in a sideslide.

Jumping the wake is one thing, but doing it in style is another. To learn the more advanced tricks—like 360s, rolls, and spins—you'll need to put in a lot of practice. You'll also have to watch and learn from others. One easy way to pick up tricks is by watching instructional wakeboarding videos. They allow you to visualize certain moves and techniques, and they're fun to watch when you can't be out on the water doing the real thing.

A great place to learn new wakeboarding tricks is at competitions. Competitions often include open instructional clinics where the pros volunteer to show you a few moves. By watching them and listening to their suggestions, you're certain to get better.

If you really want to get serious about tricks, go to a wakeboarding camp. A camp is an excellent place to get intensive one-on-one instruction. There are camps all over the country. See the Where to Play section at the end of this book for details on how to find one near you.

Beyond the Basics

More advanced wakeboarding techniques come with experience. Eventually you might even find yourself inventing your own tricks and maneuvers. The pros, who do tricks for a living, spend countless hours practicing the hardest moves. So don't expect to do anything too extreme until you've put in the time.

Trick List

Looking for a few good tricks? These are certain to make a splash:

360: Spin in a complete circle— 360 degrees—while in the air.

Dana Preble doing a 360 at the 1999 Wakeboard World Cup.

360

720: Two full spins in the air (two 360s).

Air Raley: Hit the wake and swing your body—and your board—up and over your head. Land on the opposite side of the wake, facing forward.

Air roll: Roll without using the wake.

Backside roll-to-revert: Do a backside roll, then land in fakie position.

Bonk: Intentionally hit an obstacle with the board. Wear a helmet!

Butter slide: Slide the board sideways on top of the wake.

Fakie: Riding the board backward. For a goofy-footer, this means riding or landing with the left foot forward.

Front flip: Hit the wake and flip forward, end over end.

fakie

Shaun Murray landing fakie.

front flip

Tara Hamilton doing a front flip at the 1999 Wakeboard World Cup in Orlando, Florida.

Hunter Brown doing a front roll.

front roll

Frontside roll-to-revert: Do a frontside roll, then land in fakie position.

Grind: Slide the wakeboard along an obstacle in the water. Also known as a rail-slide.

Half cab: Hit the wake in fakie position and then, as you fly over both wakes, spin 180 degrees so that when you land, you're riding forward.

Mobius: Do a backside roll with a full twist.

Moby dick: Do a tantrum with a full 360.

Nose grab: Grab the front tip of the board while airborne.

Roast beef: While flying over both wakes, reach an arm between your legs and grab the heelside of the board.

Jeff McKee, age 14, does a moby dick.

moby dick

Rob Strunharik does a nose grab at the
1998 Vans Triple Crown.

nose grab

Roll: Hit the wake and, while in the air, roll sideways so that the board goes around and over your head. A frontside roll is completed when the rider approaches the wake by carving on the toeside edge of the board. A backside roll is when the rider approaches the wake while carving with the heelside edge.

Roll-to-revert: Same as a roll except that the rider lands in fakie position.

Scarecrow: Pull a front roll, then land in fakie position.

Slob: A grab; to hold on to the board with one hand near the front foot.

Speedball: Do two complete front flips in the air.

Surface 360: Spin the board in a complete circle—360 degrees—while on the water.

Switchstance wake jump: Approach the wake in fakie position, then jump over it, landing on the other side in the same direction.

Tantrum: Hit the wake and flip backward, end over end.

Temper tantrum: Two complete tantrums in the air.

Whirlybird: A tantrum with a full 360-degree spin.

Competition

After you've mastered the basics of wakeboarding, you may decide that you want to compete. Then again, you may not. Competing is not for everyone. Many people wakeboard all their lives without ever entering a single competition.

If you do want to put your water-shredding skills to the test and have never done so before, the first thing you should do is call the World Wakeboard Association. The people at the WWA

Emily Copeland competes at the 1999 Wakeboard World Cup.

can tell you where to find amateur wakeboarding tournaments that are good for beginners. These events, which are usually open to boarders of all skill levels, often include great food, rock music, and booths where sponsors display the latest wakeboarding gear. Sometimes skill clinics are offered in which pro wakeboarders give tips and demonstrate their best tricks. Attend a skill clinic before your comp, and who knows, you might just learn the trick that wins first place!

Not all amateur tournaments are exactly the same, but there are usually

The International Amateur Waterski, Wakeboard, and Kneeboard Tour

For a little bit of friendly competition, a great place to start is with the International Amateur Waterski, Wakeboard, and Kneeboard Tour, or INT League, a series of fun events held by the International Water Sports Organization. Known as the Little League of waterskiing, the INT League promotes amateur events for wakeboarding beginners in a friendly, easygoing environment. The competitions are a great place to make new friends, demo the latest wakeboarding equipment, and work on your skills.

two major components to each competition. The first component is called freestyle. Before the freestyle event, each rider fills out what is called an attack sheet. The sheet lists the different tricks that the rider will attempt once he or she is out on the water, and it determines whether the rider will compete in the beginner, intermediate, or advanced category. If you pick the

This awesome trick is being perfomed at an amateur competion in Hood River, Oregon.

hardest tricks on the list, you'll end up competing against other advanced riders your age. Choose the easy ones, and you'll find yourself going head-to-head with other beginners. Pick carefully!

Once you're out on the water, it's time to show the judge what you've got. If you can complete all the tricks on your list and do them with style, you have a good chance of winning.

The second component to each amateur tournament is called the expression session. Each rider in the expression session is given several minutes to go out on the water and ride. Judges award points based on the difficulty and variety of tricks, how hard the rider tries, and overall style. If you make creative maneuvers on your board and catch big air, you'll earn lots of points. But whatever you do, try not to fall—the clock never stops, so you might run out of time before you can show the judges what you've got.

Once you get a taste of competition, you may get hooked. And with all the friendly people, delicious food, and screaming fans, who could blame you?

It can also be fun to watch others compete, especially the pros. Professional competitions are different from amateur ones. For one thing, these guys are really good. They're sponsored by the biggest companies in wakeboarding, and they compete for cash prizes. They throw big air and do flips, twists, and other tricks that most amateur wakeboarders wouldn't even think of trying. They seem to have been born to wakeboard, and when they're on the water, everyone watches in awe.

Judges give the pros points based on how well they complete the maneuvers, how difficult their tricks are, and how much air they catch when they hit the wakes. In the World Cup, the most prestigious professional series, the results from fifteen different tournaments are combined to determine the best male and female wakeboarders in the world. In the annual X Games wakeboarding competition, the pros gather to show the rest of the world how extreme their sport really is. And in the Olympics . . . well, wakeboarding isn't an Olympic sport just yet. That may change soon, however. Waterskiing has been accepted as a new event for the 2004 Olympic Games in Athens, Greece, and we can probably assume that wakeboarding is next. Who knows— maybe you'll be among the first Olympic competitors in wakeboarding. Go for it!

Boarder Bio

Tara Hamilton
Born:
January 16, 1982
Hometown:
Lantana, Florida

Tara Hamilton may only be in her third year as a professional wakeboarder, but she hasn't wasted any time in establishing herself as one of the sport's very best. In her 1997 rookie season, she dominated the competition while winning the X Games, the Pro Wakeboard Series, and the Wakeboard World Championships. In 1998 she won the Worlds again, proving that she's here to stay.

X-planations

bindings The straps or booties that hold your feet in place on top of the board.

boat speed The ideal boat speed for a wakeboarder is usually between eighteen and twenty-two miles per hour. The speed should be fast enough to keep the board skimming on top of the water and fast enough to make a good wake for jumping.

buoyant Able to float on water.

dock start When a rider starts in a seated or standing position on a dock. The boat pulls the rider off of the dock and into the water.

double up This is a type of wake created when the boat does a wide turn and then crosses over its old wake. When the new wake and the old wake cross each other, they combine to form one really big wake—perfect for catching huge jumps.

fakie Also known as switchstance position, this is when you ride the board backward. For goofy-footers, this means riding with the left foot forward. For regular-footers, it's riding with the right foot forward.

goofy-footers Boarders who ride with their right foot in the forward position.

heelside edge The backside of the board, where the rider's heels rest. Also known as backside edge.

life jacket An inflatable vest that will keep a person afloat in water.

shred To wakeboard skillfully and fast.

sick Cool; rad.

Skurfer   An early version of a wakeboard, which was narrower and more buoyant than today's boards and did not have bindings.

spotter   Someone who watches the wakeboarder from the boat and helps the him or her communicate with the boat's driver.

stoked   When you're "stoked," you're pumped up and psyched to ride.

toeside   This is the frontside edge of the board, where the rider's toes rest.

towrope   A rope attached to the back of the boat. The wakeboarder holds on to a handle at the other end of the rope.

wake   A wavy trail that a boat leaves behind itself as it moves through the water.

Extreme Info

Web Sites

Adventure Sports On-line
http://www.adventuresports.com

Behind the Boat On-line Magazine
http://www.behindtheboat.com

Boardfinder Auction
http://www.buy.at/boardfinder

Boat Owners World
http://www.boatowners.com

ESPN Sports Zone
http://www.espnsportszone.com/extreme/xgames/index.html

Extreme Power Sports
http://www.extremepowersports.com

Extreme Sports On-line
http://www.extreme-sports.com

Launch Wakeboarding Magazine
www.launchwake.com

L Ten
http://www.wakeworld.com/level10

Pro Wakeboard Tour
http://www.prowakeboardtour.com

Wakeboard Review
http://www.wakeboardreview.com

The Wakeboard Shop
http://www.thewakeboardshop.com

Wakeboard USA
http://www.members.xoom.com/wakebordnusa/wakeboard2.htm

Wake Canada
http://www.wakecanada.com

WakeCentral.com
http://www.wakecentral.com

WakeWorld Wakeboarding
http://www.wakeworld.com

WakeZone
http://spforever.simplenet.com/wakezone.htm

Organizations

International Water Sports Organization
P.O. Box 283
Black Diamond, WA 98010
(253) 887-1606

e-mail: anchor fun@league.com
Web site: http://www.intleague.com

Pro Wakeboard Tour
World Sports & Marketing
P.O. Box 2456
Winter Park, FL 32790
Phone: (407) 628-4802
Fax: (407) 628-7061
e-mail: protour@worldzine.com
Web site: http://www.prowakeboardtour.com

USA Water Ski
799 Overton Drive
Winter Haven, FL 33884
Phone: (941) 325-4341
Fax: (941) 325-8259
Web site: http://www.awsa.com

World Wakeboard Association (WWA)
689 Old Berkley Road
Auburndale, FL 33823
(941) 984-3750

Where to Play

Camps and Schools

There are many wakeboarding camps across the country. To find one in your area, check the WakeWorld Web site or contact *Wake Boarding* magazine. Here are a few camps to get you started:

Boarding School
4551 FM 660
Ferris, TX 75125
(972) 842-2645
Web site: http://www.boardingschool.com

Discovery Bay Wakeboard and Ski Center
5901 Marina Road, Suite 3
Byron, CA 94514
Phone: (800) 266-7789
Fax: (925) 634-3125
e-mail: companyinfo@h20skiya.com
Web site: http://www.h20skiya.com

Hansen Ski Center
P.O. Box 216
Groveland, FL 34736
(352) 429-3574
e-mail: skihansen@aol.com

Lone Star Wakeboard Camp and Water Ski School
Route 1, Box 259D
Highway 71 East
Smithville, TX 78957
(512) 360-2222
Web site: http://www.golonestar.com

Orlando International Waterski Center
8505 West Irlo Bronson Memorial Highway (Hwy. 192)
Kissimmee, FL 34746
(407) 654-9292

O-Town WaterSports Wakeboard School
5220 East Colonial Drive
Orlando, FL 32807
(407) 380-0734
e-mail: otown@magicnet.net

The Wakeboard Camp
931 West Montrose
Clermont, FL 34711
(352) 394-8899
e-mail: wbored@aol.com
Web site: http://www.wakeboardcamp.com

World Wakeboard Center
P.O. Box 216
Groveland, FL 34736
Phone: (352) 429-3574
Fax: (352) 429-2091
e-mail: skihansen1@aol.com
Web site: http://www.skibenzel.com

Competitions

The major professional wakeboarding competition is the Wakeboard World Cup. The events in the World Cup series include the X Games, the Wakeboard Nationals, the Wakeboard World Championships, the Pro Wakeboard Tour events, Vans Triple Crown of Wakeboarding, and the invitation-only Masters series. The World Wakeboard Association oversees all World Cup events.

For information on amateur competitions, check with your local sports shop, visit the Web sites listed in the Extreme Info section, or contact the International Water Sports Organization.

Extreme Reading

Books

McKenna, Anne T. *Extreme Wakeboarding*. Mankato, MN: Capstone Press, 1999.

McManners, Hugh. *Water Sports: An Outdoor Adventure Handbook*. New York: DK Publishing, 1997.

Waterski staff. *Boating Watersports: The Ultimate Get Started Guide to Towing Fun*. Winter Park, FL: World Publications, 1990.

Magazines

Wake Boarding
330 West Canton Avenue
Winter Park, FL 32792
(407) 628-4802;
e-mail: subscribe@wakeboardingmag.com
Web site: http://www.world.pub.net

Wake Boarding magazine is the only magazine in the world devoted entirely to the sport of wakeboarding. In addition to radical photographs of the sport's top stars attempting their hardest tricks, the magazine includes articles on the latest developments in wakeboarding equipment, from boards to bindings to boats.

CD-ROM

Schwartz, Bill. Interactive Guide to Wake Boarding. Orlando, FL: Interactive Media Productions, 1998.

To find a local or mail-order dealer that carries this CD-ROM, contact:
Interactive Media Productions
5172 Stratemeyer Drive
Orlando, FL 32839
Phone: (407) 859-9059
Fax: (407) 898-7793
e-mail: imp@magicnet.net
Web site: http://www.impsports.com/imphome.htm

Index

A
attack sheet, 49

B
boating license, 22
Bonifay, Parks, 14
buoyancy, 9, 12

C
camps, 19, 36
clubs, 19
competitions, 6, 10, 14, 15, 31, 36, 47, 48, 50
    Olympics, 6, 15, 50, 51
    Pro Wakeboard Tour, 14, 15, 31, 32, 51
    Wakeboard World Championships, 31, 51
    Wakeboard World Cup, 14-15, 50
    X Games, 6, 14, 50, 51
Copeland, Emily, 32

D
demo equipment, 25-26, 48
driver, 22,-23, 24, 34

E
expression session, 31, 50

F
Finn, Tony, 11–12
freestyle, 48–49

G
gear, 19, 22, 25–30, 47
    bindings, 9, 11, 18, 21, 25, 28–29, 33
    boards, twin-tip, 13, 27
    boat, finding a, 18, 26
    extended pylon, 30
    "fat sack," 30
    life jacket/preserver, 18, 21, 22, 25
    towrope/towline, 20, 21, 25, 29–30, 34, 36
    wet suit, 30
goofy-foot, 33, 38

H
Hamilton, Tara, 51
hand signals, 22, 24
heelside, 35, 42, 45
Hyperlite, 12–13

I
International Water Sports Organization, 48
INT League, 48

L
laws, 17–18, 22

M
Murray, Shaun, 31

N
"no wake" rules, 23

O

O'Brien, Herb, 12
obstacles, 23, 38, 42

P

Pascoe, Mike and Mark, 11–12
practice, 19, 32, 36
professionals, 13, 14, 15, 30, 31, 36, 48, 50, 51

R

regular-foot, 33

S

safety, 8, 21, 22, 24
skill clinics, 36, 48
skills, 7, 11, 47, 48
Skurfer, 11–12
snowboarding, 4, 9, 12, 33
speed, 4, 6, 8, 10, 22
spotter, 22, 34
style, 28, 49, 50

T

techniques, 7, 32, 36
television coverage, 7, 15
toeside, 35, 45
tournaments, amateur, 18, 19, 25–26, 47, 48, 49
tricks, 4, 5, 10, 20, 27, 28, 29, 30, 32, 36, 38, 48, 49, 50
   air Raley, 21, 38
   bunny hop, 36
   "fakie," 27, 38, 42, 45
   flips, 5, 42, 45, 46, 50
   jumps, 4, 10, 12, 35–36, 45
   rolls, 4, 5, 36, 38, 42, 45
   spins, 4, 5, 10, 36, 38, 45, 46
   tantrum, 4, 46

twists, 10, 50
turns, carving, 8, 9, 19, 35

W

Wake Boarding magazine, 14, 19
waterskiing, 4, 6, 12, 13, 15, 16, 17, 18–19, 23, 30, 32, 48, 51
windsurfing, 6, 11–12
World Wakeboard Association (WWA), 13–14, 15, 19, 47

Credits

Chris Hayhurst is a freelance writer and photographer who specializes in the outdoors, sports, and environmental issues. In his spare time, he enjoys hiking, rock climbing, telemark skiing, and anything that takes him into the backcountry. He lives in Santa Fe, New Mexico.

Photo Credits

Cover photo © Stephan Hunziker/Sports Chrome USA; pp. 4, 10, 13, 14, 16, 20, 23, 24, 25, 26, 30, 31, 32, 33, 37, 41, 43, 44, 47, & 51 © Heather Lee; p. 5 © AdamPretty/Allsport; p. 7 © CORBIS/Neil Rabinowitz; pp. 9, 11 & 29 © CORBIS/Rick Doyle; pp. 12, 34, 39, 40 & 41 © Doug Dukane; p. 13 © Erik Aeder; pp. 18 & 27 by Thaddeus Harden; p. 21 © Tom King; p. 35 © Richard Martin/Agence Vandystadt; p. 49 © Eric Sanford/Mountain Stock

Special thanks to New York Pipe Dreams for allowing us to use their store for the photos on pages 18 and 27.

Series Design

Oliver Halsman Rosenberg

Layout

Laura Murawski

Consulting Editor

Amy Gelman Haugesag